t i a

To all readers,

Thank you for choosing our book. This book was first published in Japan in 2019 after we had warmed the concept for two years. Since the book was published, I have felt the significant impacts and changes in many families by this story. People told me, "The story makes our family think about everyday's life together." "We are choosing bananas with Fairtrade Marks." "My children asked a question about ethical consumption to store staff." As we hope more and more people will encounter this story, we decided to publish the English translation.

What is remarkable for this version is that it was translated by students of International Christian University. Instead of working on the translation immediately, the students started with learning about ethical consumption to deeply understand the context of the story and the implication of each word. Through their efforts, they have given this book a new life. It is astonishing how lively their translation sounds, which has exceeded my expectation. I hope you can also sense the spirits of the 24 students as you read the words they have chosen to translate this story.

As I believe that intergenerational equity is absolutely essential to shape a more ethical society, I am happy that I have been able to work with the youth, who will forge the future, to deliver the idea and value of ethicality to the world through this book. I would like to express my deep appreciation for the ICU students, Professor Tatsuo Nunoshiba, Professor Beverley Curran, the publisher Yamakawa Shuppansha, and experts who have made the translation of this book possible.

The future is in our hands – let's become part of the solution, not the problem. Be the change!

May 2020,
on a serene day in the beginning of summer

Rika Sueyoshi

JN080774

Can you imagine when our planet was born?
It dates back to 4.6 billion years ago.
And it is said that 3.8 billion years ago,
the origin of life started.

It's a longer history than you think.

Since then, life has evolved,
and 200 thousand years ago, Homo sapiens,
yes, you humans, appeared.

The earth is
in danger.

Off you go little one.
Go ahead and tell
the humans.

And soon, humans created fire, developed languages and
lived together.
They plowed the land and grew crops.
The humans matured.
And their lifestyles changed through many discoveries and
inventions.

Life for humans became convenient with the introduction of
money, machines and electricity.
But because humans didn't care about limits,
their behavior has brought bad effects on the air, water,
forests, soil and even the animals.

As you may already know,
our planet is in a critical condition now.
After we reach the tipping point, there is no going back.

This book is for all of you living in this era...

Oh, me?

Are You Ready?
The Journey to the Veiled World

Rika Sueyoshi   Gaku Nakagawa

Translated by
Students from International Christian University

Munch munch

    I love bananas!

        I eat them every single day.

Do you love bananas, too?

    Can you guess how these bananas are produced?

            I'll show you if you don't know!

Are You Ready?
Go ethical and beyond !
Take us to the world under the veil !

POP!

Here we are in the Philippines,
a hot country in Southeast Asia.
There is a large farm called a plantation,
covered with only banana trees as far as
the eye can see.
There had been a jungle where my friends used to live,
but now no one lives here.

wHOOOOSH! WATCH OUT!

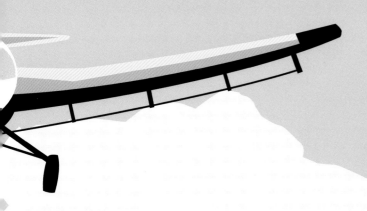

The airplane is spreading chemicals
to prevent bugs and diseases.

People are living and going to school
right next to the plantation.
They are breathing in the chemicals,
which makes them sick.

You may eat bananas raised like that.

This is the real story of the veiled world,
the planet that we all live on.

Let's go to another farm
in the same country, the Philippines.
Can you hear the lively voice of
farmers and kids?

There are a lot of bananas
grown in this mountain.
Because farmers do not use
chemicals on this farm,
all the trees look healthy.

Farmers have to carry
heavy bananas off of the mountain,
but they seem to have fun.
Look, they are washing off
bugs and dirt by hand.

These bananas, grown so carefully, must be so delicious!

YUMMY!

Next is a story from the world of the ocean.
What do you think this huge fish is?

The fish that may soon disappear from this world.
It's tuna, your favorite.

But think about it.
You see tuna lined up on supermarket shelves and
served in sushi restaurants.
Yet, why do you think they will disappear soon?

I'll show you if you don't know!

Go ethical and beyond !
Take us to the world under the veil !

POP!

oh, no!

Here we are in the middle of the Pacific Ocean.

Look, fishermen are catching tunas.
Even a lot of baby tunas are caught in the net.

Round and round.
Tunas are spinning around.
"Pull it up!", a fisherman said.

In a blink,
so many fish were pulled out of the water!
If humans say "we want more" and
keep catching too many tunas,
they will disappear from the earth.

This is the real story of the veiled world,
the planet that we all live on.

But there are other ways to fish, too.

Some fishermen carefully decide
when and how much to fish
so that fish will not disappear from the ocean.

You can find fish caught by
such fishermen in supermarkets.

Hey hey, little monkey,
What do you mean by "ethical and beyond"?

Good question!

It's a magic spell that anyone can use.

Using this spell, we can unveil the world.

Do you want to know
the secret behind the magic spell?
Then let's continue
the journey together!

Come on, where do you think
the next destination is?

Go ethical and beyond!
Take us to the world under the veil!

POP!

Here we are in Ghana, a country in West Africa.

This is a farm of cacao beans,
which chocolate is made from.
Heave ho, they are carrying big cacao pods
shaped like rugby balls.

Hold on. Are children working there?

How dangerous that they are using sharp,
broad-bladed knives!
Because they carry heavy pods on their head,
their entire bodies hurt.
Even if they get tired or ill, they cannot ask for a break.
The family is too poor to survive without the children's help.

Even if they work hard, they cannot earn much.
In fact, very few children here have eaten chocolate before.

This is the real story of the veiled world,
the planet that we all live on.

Let's look at another cacao farm.

See? Cacao beans are growing in the forest.
Coconuts and pineapples are growing, too.
We can harvest many kinds of food on this farm.

Plants are raised without chemicals,
so forests are lively as they should be.

Here, children do not have to work.
Because adults earn enough for
the whole family to live comfortably.

For the people, the forest,
and the animals living there,
this chocolate makes everyone happy.

The journey must go on.

Here we are in India, a country in South Asia.

Farmers are making cotton for T-shirts and towels.
They spray tons of chemicals to prevent bugs
from damaging the cotton.
But chemicals pollute the soil and rivers, and make people ill.

In India, it is said that cotton farmers can only live 35 years
on average.
Unable to repay the money borrowed for seeds and chemicals,
some are driven to kill themselves.

Even children are working.

Although the boiling-hot weather and
chemicals make them feel sick,
they can't quit their job.
They can't go to school, even if they want to.

This is the real story of the veiled world,
the planet that we all live on.

POP!

Here we go!
It's almost the end of our journey.

Next is about something we all know well.
Have you thought about how, by whom,
and where your clothes are made?

I'll show you if you don't know!

Go ethical and beyond !
Take us to the world under the veil!

Here we are in Bangladesh,
a small country in South Asia.

In a factory, many people are sewing
from dawn to dusk.

They are packed into a room and working
more than 14 hours a day to make clothes.
They are sweating and exhausted.
Even worse, no one can drink clean water.

But, they earn just a little money.

Even if the walls have cracks and
the building is about to collapse,
they have no choice but to
keep making clothes without complaints.

Do you know why? Because many of
you want to buy a lot at a cheap price.

This is the real story of the veiled world,
the planet that we all live on.

How about another factory in the same country, Bangladesh?

Bright sunlight and soothing breeze fill the room where
workers are weaving carefully.
Once the fabric is made, they put patterns with
large wooden stamps.
Then, they cut and sew to make the fabric into clothes.

All the workers look happy with their job.
They enjoy their lunchtime and go home when it gets dark.
Also, they earn enough money for their families.

Wouldn't it be wonderful to wear the clothes made in
such a factory?

Alright! Let's go up up above the clouds.
Hold on tight!

Can you see the tiger? The elephant?
The rhino? The snake? The polar bears?
The eagle? The owl? The salmon?
The bee? The leopard?
These are just some of the animals
that might be gone in the near future.

Someday, we monkeys might also be gone from the earth.
The precious forest that we call our home, too.
All we can do is to live in this world given by you.

But you know what?
One thing is for sure. You can make this world a better place.

When you eat bananas or fish, or buy some chocolate or clothes, you can choose the ones that make humans and animals happy.

Your choices will shape the future of our planet.

This is the end of the real story of the veiled world.

But, wait a minute! There's more!
Behind many things, other than chocolate, fish, or clothes,
the real story of the veiled world exists too.

When you start to hear that story,
remember to say the magical spell!

Go ethical and beyond !
Take us to the world under the Veil !

FARMERS
MARKET

FRESH
FISH

Yes, "Go ethical and beyond!"
This means that you have the power to unveil the world.

There are many veiled things around us
that you are going to see.

Let's say, why is the earth becoming warmer?
Think about what we saw in our journey.
Say those words, find your answers.

Now it's time to say good-bye.

So, it's your turn to start a new journey.

You can start from where you are.

At home, at school, in the city you are living,
with your family and all of your friends!

Are You Ready?
Go ethical and beyond !
Take us to the world under the veil !

You can find these labels
on food products that are produced
naturally without chemicals.

【 JAS 】

【 Regulation EEC. No.834/
2007 of Organic Production 】

【 USDA 】

You can find this label
on foods and drinks
produced with care for
forests and workers.

【 Rainforest Alliance 】

You can find
this label on palm oil
produced with care for
nature and society.

【 RSPO 】

You can find these labels
on fish and shells caught
with care for clean water
and marine life.

【 MSC 】

【 ASC 】

【 JAS 】
Organic label for the food products produced or processed
under the production basis mandated by the JAS law. This
label ensures that the certified products are produced
naturally.

【 Regulation EEC. No.834/2007 of Organic Production 】
Organic label for the European Union member countries. The
EU and Japan acknowledge the equivalent level of quality of
each other's organic certification scheme.

【 USDA 】
Organic label certified by the U.S. Department of Agriculture.
The U.S. and Japan acknowledge the equivalent level of
quality of each other's organic certification scheme.

【 RSPO 】
Certification label for products with palm oil that is produced
sustainably so as not to negatively affect rainforests,
biodiversity, and people's lives, or products that contribute
to the production of sustainable palm oil.

【 Rainforest Alliance 】
Certification label given to products made with produce from
farms which meet the standard of sustainable agriculture.

【 MSC 】
Certification label given to fishery products caught with
environmental considerations.

【 ASC 】
Certification label given only to fishery products that are
produced through farming with consideration for the
environment and society.

**Look for these labels
when you shop!
You can find them on the tags,
bags or boxes of items.**

There are many other labels, too. Let's find and learn about them!

You can find these labels
on products made by workers whose
human rights are protected.

GUARANTEED
FAIR TRADE
【 WFTO Label 】

【 Fairtrade Marks 】

FAIR TRADE
CERTIFIED™
【 Fairtrade USA 】

You can find these labels
on textile products that
are made from organically
grown fibers.

【 GOTS 】

【 OCS 】

You can find this label
on wooden products and
paper to protect
the forest.

【 FSC® 】

【 GOTS 】
Certification label given to organic textile products. It requires to use at least 70% organic fiber, use no harmful chemicals, and ensure environmentally and socially good conditions for workers.

【 OCS 】
Certification label for organic fiber products which verifies that a final product contains the accurate amount of a given organically grown material by tracking the supply chain.

【 FSC® 】
Certification label by Forest Stewardship Council (FSC) which verifies that forest products are made with trees in forests managed in a way that preserves biological diversity, local people and workers.

【 Fairtrade Marks 】
Certification Mark that assures fairtrade among the producers, and shows that the product was produced with the protection of human rights and safety towards the environment.

【 WFTO Label 】
Label that shows that the practices across the supply chain are checked against the WFTO Fair Trade Standard, and that products are made and traded by Guaranteed Fair Trade Organisations.

【 Fairtrade USA 】
Certification label that shows that the strict societal, environmental and economical standards are followed. The certification also assures a safe working environment, protection of the natural environment, sustainable life, and support for community improvement (premium).

Supervision: Japan Sustainable Labels Association

Afterword by the Translators

This English translation was created by student volunteers at International Christian University (as of 2019). We would like to once again thank the author, Ms. Rika Sueyoshi, and Ms. Rie Hirai, the editorial department of Yamakawa Shuppansha Ltd. for trusting us in our translation work.

What brought ICU students to join this English translation? A few years ago, one of the translation project members joined Ms. Sueyoshi's fair trade study course, when she started to pay attention to "the veiled world." To discuss ethical consumption together, we invited Ms. Sueyoshi to our university. As it was right after her picture book had been published, we came up with the idea of this translation project.

We started our translation by learning the translation methods and ethical consumption. There is a diversity of words and we tried to expand our creativity to convey the author's intention. At the same time, we studied together to understand what is happening in our world and how people are trying to make it better.

This project allowed us to learn a lot. Translation is not only changing the original texts automatically into another language – it is also possible to weave our ideas into texts. As students majoring in various disciplines were working on the project together, our broad perspectives made translation thicker.

We believe that this story will inspire the world. As part of the younger generation, we are aware that our actions can make a difference. As well as children, all generations can enjoy and learn from the story. We hope that you can share the time with people who you care about, and have a dialogue about this story. By doing so, we can understand the veiled world and imagine people in different situations.
This story might become a milestone for you to think about your everyday life and start taking action. In the end, we can make a huge impact on the world.

That said, what can individuals do to make the world a better place? This story tells us that as consumers we are responsible for carefully choosing what to buy. Checking labels to make sure the products are fairly traded, organically grown, and/or locally made is one of the easiest steps to change our habit of consumption.

As well as buying such products, we believe that "not consuming" is also a part of ethical consumption. By carrying a reusable water bottle and shopping bag, we can reduce waste in our daily life. By repairing broken items, we can use them longer. Like this, it's also important to think before buying something if we really need it.

As the monkey in the book said, "you can start from where you are" — you don't have to be a perfectly ethical consumer. In fact, there's no such thing as perfection! What's important for each one of us is that we try to take action that is better for people, animals and the planet, no matter how small it may be. Because our future will be shaped by our everyday choices and actions. Through these actions, we hope our future will be fairer for people and in harmony with nature. Are you ready for a journey with us to make it happen? Go ethical and beyond!

April 2020

Momona, Hana, and Riho
from the ICU translation team

Acknowledgements

This translation was made possible thanks to the support from many people and organizations. We would especially like to thank the author Ms. Rika Sueyoshi, the editor Ms. Rie Hirai, and Professor Tatsuo Nunoshiba for supporting our project, Professor Beverley Curran for teaching us the basic tips of translation, Ms. Yuko Tayanagi from Action against Child Exploitation, Ms. Komomo Tanba, Ms. Sayaka Nakanishi and Mr. Takayuki Tsujii for sharing the knowledge about child labor and sustainability in fashion.

Student Volunteers from
International Christian University

Ai Chijiwa	Aoka Kudo
Asako Jindo	Ayumi Oshita
Hana Matsuo	Himawari Morita
Kanako Matsuyama	Kei Takahashi
Kentaro Nunokawa	Kiko Asano
Mano Mori	Mika Nishitani
Miki Takahashi	Minami Hirata
Mizuki Okawa	Mizuki Matsumura
Momona Otsuka	Natsumi Kato
Riho Matsumaru	Rino Motomura
Sae Shima	Satsuki Tateno
Sonomi Tsuruta	Tomoko Matsunaga

Rika Sueyoshi

Rika Sueyoshi is one of many people who have been seeking a way of society that can coexist with nature, since realizing the downside of capitalism. She is the Representative Director of the Ethical Association, and has organized seminars, events and workshops for local governments, companies and educational institutions to raise awareness of ethical consumption.

little monkey

I am a little monkey. Along with rules of nature, I am living wholeheartedly as well as many other monkeys.
I am here to have humans realize their impacts on the earth. In order to do so, my dad gave me the magical power; to see, hear, and speak the truth.
That is why everyone calls me a wise monkey who unveils the world.

Gaku Nakagawa

Gaku Nakagawa is a Buddhist priest based in Kyoto who also works as an illustrator internationally. He decided to join the making of this picture book after finding the concept of ethical consumption similar to Buddhist thinking, which is to resist human desire and live with care for the natural environment and the socially weak. One of his well-known works is *The World's Poorest President Speaks Out.*

Are You Ready?
The Journey to the Veiled World

Print Date   10th August 2020
Issue Date   20th August 2020

Written by   Rika Sueyoshi
Illustrated by   Gaku Nakagawa
Translated by   Students from
                International Christian University

Publisher   Shimpei Nozawa

Publishing   Yamakawa Shuppansha Ltd.
1-13-13 Uchikanda Chiyoda-ku Tokyo 101-0047 Japan
Tel 81 3-3293-8131   Fax 81 3-3293-8130
URL www.yamakawa.co.jp

Printing and Bound   Okamura Printing Industries Co.,Ltd.

Are You Ready?

2020年8月10日　第1版第1刷印刷
2020年8月20日　第1版第1刷発行

文　末吉里花

絵　中川 学

訳　国際基督教大学 翻訳プロジェクト

発行者　野澤伸平

発行所　株式会社山川出版社
〒101-0047 東京都千代田区内神田1-13-13
電話 03-3293-8131（営業）　1802（編集）
https://www.yamakawa.co.jp/ ／振替 00120-9-43993

印刷・製本　岡村印刷工業株式会社

FSC
www.fsc.org

MIX
Paper from
responsible sources
FSC™ C020779